Landmark
Events in
American
History

Lexington
and Concord

Michael V. Uschan

WORLD ALMANAC® LIBRARY

For Kallen DeBack

3 3113 02115 0976

Please visit our web site at: www.worldalmanaclibrary.com
For a free color catalog describing World Almanac® Library's list of high-quality
books and multimedia programs, call 1-800-848-2928 (USA) or 1-800-387-3178
(Canada). World Almanac® Library's fax: (414) 332-3567.

Library of Congress Cataloging-in-Publication Data

Uschan, Michael V., 1948-
    Lexington and Concord / by Michael V. Uschan.
        p. cm. — (Landmark events in American history)
    Summary: Describes the first battles of the Revolutionary War, their causes, and consequences.
    Includes bibliographical references and index.
    ISBN 0-8368-5379-2 (lib. bdg.)
    ISBN 0-8368-5407-1 (softcover)
    1. Lexington, Battle of, Lexington, Mass., 1775—Juvenile literature. 2. Concord, Battle of,
Concord, Mass., 1775—Juvenile literature. [1. Lexington, Battle of, Lexington, Mass., 1775.
2. Concord, Battle of, Concord, Mass., 1775. 3. United States—History—Revolution, 1775-
1783—Campaigns.] I. Title. II. Series.
E241.L6U73 2003
973.3'311—dc21   2003047923

First published in 2004 by
World Almanac® Library
330 West Olive Street, Suite 100
Milwaukee, WI 53212 USA

Produced by Discovery Books
Editor: Sabrina Crewe
Designer and page production: Sabine Beaupré
Photo researcher: Sabrina Crewe
Maps and diagrams: Stefan Chabluk
World Almanac® Library editorial direction: Mark J. Sachner
World Almanac® Library art direction: Tammy Gruenewald
World Almanac® Library production: Beth Meinholz and Jessica Yanke

Photo credits: Corbis: cover, pp. 4, 5, 9, 10, 11, 12, 15, 16, 17, 19, 20, 21, 23, 24,
26, 27, 28, 29, 30, 31, 32, 33, 34, 35, 36, 39, 40, 41, 42, 43; The Granger Collection:
pp. 7, 22, 37; Library of Congress: pp. 9, 14, 18; National Park Service, Colonial
National Historical Park: p. 6.

Printed in the United States of America

1 2 3 4 5 6 7 8 9 07 06 05 04 03

Contents

Introduction   4

Chapter 1: The British Colonies   6

Chapter 2: Moving Toward Rebellion   14

Chapter 3: At Lexington and Concord   24

Chapter 4: The War for Independence   32

Chapter 5: A New Kind of Government   38

Conclusion   42

Time Line   44

Glossary   45

Further Information   46

Index   47

Introduction

The War Begins

The first shots of the American Revolution were fired on April 19, 1775, at Lexington and Concord, two towns in Massachusetts. The shots came in brief, bloody clashes between British soldiers and American **Minutemen**, volunteer soldiers who had risen up against the British king and government.

Why They Fought

The shots that made history that chilly spring morning marked the beginning of the break between the men, women, and children who lived in thirteen British **colonies** and the country that ruled them from thousands of miles away. The colonists had once considered themselves loyal British subjects, but they now thought of themselves as Americans. They had been edging toward rebellion for several years.

Colonists began to turn against Britain because they believed that the powerful nation was ruling them unfairly.

The clashes that made up the Battle of Lexington and Concord are still remembered today. These men are reenacting the incident on Lexington Green in which the first shots of the American Revolution were fired.

The split grew when King George III and the British **Parliament** refused to respond to colonists' complaints about how they were governed.

An Important Event

Lexington and Concord was the first battle of the American Revolution. To the amazement of the entire world, the upstart Americans declared independence and defeated Britain in the war to claim the colonies as their own.

Thanks to "Concord Hymn," a famous poem by Ralph Waldo Emerson, the first shot fired by Americans at the British on North Bridge at Concord is known as the "shot heard 'round the world." However, it was not the sound of a gun going off that began to echo around the world. Instead, it was the power of the new nation's ideals—those of **natural rights** and a **republican** form of government—that resounded for many years to come.

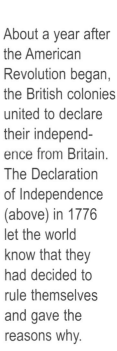

About a year after the American Revolution began, the British colonies united to declare their independence from Britain. The Declaration of Independence (above) in 1776 let the world know that they had decided to rule themselves and gave the reasons why.

Founding a Republic

The United States of America was founded as a republic. A republic is a nation with a head of state who is not a **monarch**, but somebody chosen by citizens or their representatives. The head of state and other elected officials make decisions about how the country is run. This was a bold idea in the 1770s. In most countries, monarchs ruled and ordinary people had little say in the governing of their nations. Only a minority of adult Americans had the right to vote as citizens of the republic when the new nation was formed, however. Most Americans—for instance women, Native Americans, and African Americans—could not vote.

The British Colonies

The first British settlement that lasted any length of time was Jamestown in Virginia. From its earliest days, shown here, the colony always struggled to survive.

A Fruitful Land

"Within is a country that may have the [advantage] over the most pleasant places known, for large and pleasant navigable rivers, heaven and earth never agreed better to frame a place for man's habitations. Here are mountains, hills, plains, valleys, rivers, brooks, all running most pleasantly into a fair bay [Chesapeake Bay] and surrounded with fruitful and delightsome land."

Captain John Smith,
Jamestown settler, 1624

The First of the Colonies

On May 14, 1607, a group of 105 men and boys from England landed in North America on the coast of what is now Virginia. There, they established the settlement of Jamestown as the capital of the colony of Virginia.

Virginia was the first of the thirteen British colonies that would become the United States of America. It was established by the Virginia Company, a group of investors who put up the money to found the colony. They hoped to profit from the colony by selling what the colonists grew or produced.

The settlers who came to Jamestown struggled to survive. Virginia Governor George Percy wrote of the colony's beginning: "There were never Englishmen left in a foreign country in such misery." This was in part because the colonists lacked the skills to provide themselves with food, but they also died in large numbers from disease, and some were killed in battles with Native Americans. Of about 7,300 people who moved to Virginia between 1607 and 1624, more than 6,000 died.

More Colonies Are Created

A group of Puritan Separatists, later known as the "Pilgrims," landed at Plymouth on December 21, 1620, to begin a colony that was absorbed a few years later into the larger Puritan colony of Massachusetts. (Puritans were those who wished to "purify" the Church of England, and the Separatists were so called because they had separated altogether from the Church of England.) The Massachusetts colony, as well as being a religious community, was also a business venture for

The Pilgrims receive farming advice from Squanto (center), whose people lived at Plymouth —then called Patuxet—before the English colonists arrived in 1620.

The First Americans

When colonists arrived in North America in the 1600s, they encountered the land's original inhabitants. Millions of Native Americans—whom the white settlers called "Indians"—had lived there for thousands of years. Some Native people were friendly at first and taught colonists how to hunt game and grow American crops, such as corn. But in every colony, Native Americans and colonists soon began to fight each other. Colonists took land away from Indians, forced some to become slaves, and used superior weapons to dominate them. The battle to take Native land and wipe out the Indian population would continue for more than two centuries.

its investors. Its population grew quickly in the mid-1600s, and people began moving to nearby areas, creating the colonies of Rhode Island, Connecticut, and New Hampshire. North Carolina, South Carolina, and Pennsylvania were founded when English kings granted large areas of land in eastern North America to their political supporters.

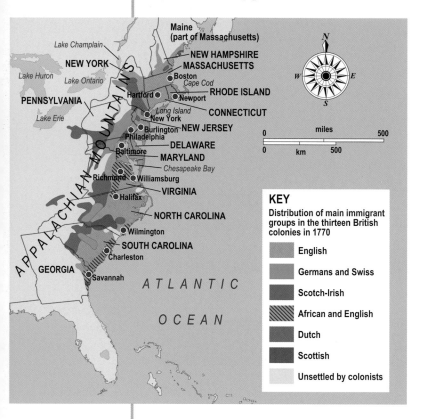

Why Colonists Came

Colonists had many reasons for coming to their new land. One motive was religion, as was the case in the Puritan colonies, where people arrived to join communities based on their particular religious beliefs. Lord Baltimore founded Maryland as a haven for Roman Catholics, who were frequently persecuted in Europe. Rhode Island, established in 1636, was the first North American colony to offer religious freedom, a place where people of all religions could find acceptance.

Gradually, a chain of colonies grew up along the Atlantic coast. In 1733, more than a century after Virginia was founded, Georgia became the thirteenth British colony in North America.

The Chance to Own Land

Colonists also came in search of a better life. The great goal of colonists was to own land—something only the rich could do in Europe—and most colonies gave land to people willing to face the difficulties and settle there. As one North Carolina colonist said in 1711, "The land is good but the beginning is hard."

Many men and women could not afford to pay the fare to North America. In order to get there, they signed contracts as **indentured servants**. This meant they had to work as virtual slaves for other colonists for several years in exchange for the cost of the journey across the Atlantic Ocean.

The Colonies Develop

In the 1600s and 1700s, thousands of colonists came from the European countries of Germany, the Netherlands, Sweden, and France. The vast majority of the colonists, however, were from Great Britain (comprising England, Wales, and Scotland) or British-ruled Ireland. Because of this, the English language and British political and social customs became standard.

Education was very important to the settlers of New England in the 1700s. This primer—an elementary reading and spelling book —belonged to Lucy Wadsworth of Connecticut.

How Colonies Were Governed

The British colonies in North America were owned by the British monarch and ruled from Britain. The British Parliament passed laws affecting the trade and foreign affairs of its colonies, and it appointed a governor for each colony. Colonists in North America, unlike other British citizens, were not allowed to vote in elections for Parliament and had no say in choosing their governors.

Each colony elected members to a **legislature** that made laws for its region, and colonists pretty much governed themselves with regard to internal affairs. But when British governors and colonial legislatures disagreed on major issues, the governors had the power to overturn decisions of legislators.

Britain imposed taxes on the colonists to raise money for local government and for the costs of keeping British soldiers in North America. American colonists paid lower taxes than other British citizens, and in practice their taxes were often not collected at all.

In the Middle Colonies, large cities such as Philadelphia and New York grew up along with many medium-sized cities. New York, shown here in its early days, was originally a Dutch city, and from the mid-1600s, it had a diverse and multinational population.

Despite the English influence that was common to all, however, the various colonies began to develop their own characteristics and economies. These differences were great enough to create three distinct regions: New England, the Middle Colonies, and the Southern Colonies. The two Chesapeake Colonies—Virginia and Maryland—are often included in the Southern Colonies.

Three Separate Regions

New England included the northernmost colonies of New Hampshire, Massachusetts, Rhode Island, and Connecticut. People who settled there were almost entirely from English stock. Most were farmers, but many became merchants or manufacturers. Others made their living from the sea, either by fishing or by shipping goods to and from other countries. New England had many towns but only one really large city, Boston.

The Middle Colonies—New York, Pennsylvania, New Jersey, and Delaware—had more cities and attracted more people from other European countries, especially from Germany. Although farming was the main occupation, these colonies also developed lumber, fur, and grain-processing industries.

The Southern Colonies —Virginia, Maryland, North Carolina, South Carolina, and Georgia—were very different from the other two regions. Life there was more rural. There were few large towns, and almost everyone worked in agriculture of some kind. The desire for cheap labor on their tobacco and cotton plantations led the wealthier white Southerners to buy many Africans as slaves. By the mid-1700s, there were about 400,000 slaves in the South.

Marking Out the Town

"I went myself to the Savannah River. I fixed upon a healthy Situation about Ten Miles from the Sea. The River here forms a Half-Moon, along the south side of which the Banks are about Forty Feet high, and on the Top a Flag, which they call a Bluff. I have marked out the Town and Common; half of the former is already cleared and the first House was begun Yesterday in the Afternoon."

James Oglethorpe, first governor of Georgia, describing the founding of Savannah on February 1, 1733

Life in the South was dominated by the farming of cotton and tobacco. Using the forced labor of African-American slaves, landowners grew these cash crops on large plantations.

A drawing of the British Houses of Parliament in Westminster, London, in the late 1700s. After independence, U.S. leaders used the idea of two Houses of Parliament (the Lords and the Commons) as a basis for **Congress**, which was similarly divided into the Senate and House of Representatives.

War with France

In the colonial era, Britain provided its colonies with military protection against the rival colonial powers of France and Spain. The colonies needed Britain's military might from 1754 to 1763 during a war between Britain and France. This war—called the French and Indian War by the British because of the many Native peoples that supported the French—was the culmination of decades of hostility between France and Britain in Europe and in North America, which both nations wanted to control.

The French and Indian War began in 1754, when a young **militia** leader, George Washington, and his small band of Virginia soldiers clashed with French and Native American forces in the Ohio River Valley. Washington had been ordered to stop the French from settling in the area.

Washington, who would later lead the Americans to victory over Britain, fought alongside British soldiers in the war. He wrote to his mother about one dangerous battle: "I had four bullets through my coat and two horses shot under me."

European Rivals

Britain was the most successful European nation in colonizing North America, but the British were not the first colonists to arrive. In about the year 1000, Vikings from Europe were probably the first Europeans to reach North America and found a settlement. Italian explorer Christopher Columbus came to North America in 1492, opening North and South America to colonization and exploitation by the Spanish. The French came to North America in the 1500s, and in 1608, Frenchman Samuel Champlain founded the settlement that would later become Quebec. In 1625, the Dutch settled New Amsterdam, now named New York and one of the world's major cities. The Russians reached Alaska in 1741 and founded settlements there and farther south.

A British Victory

The fighting soon spread to all the British colonies. The British eventually won the French and Indian War, which was formally ended by the 1763 Treaty of Paris. Under this treaty, France granted Britain possession of a huge tract of land extending west to the Mississippi River. Britain also acquired Florida from Spain, a French ally. Wrote historian Francis Parkman: "Half the continent had changed hands with the scratch of a pen."

The maps below show how the North American continent was divided up among rival colonial powers before (left) and after (right) the 1763 Treaty of Paris. Britain acquired land to the west and south of its thirteen colonies.

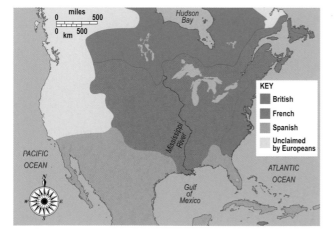

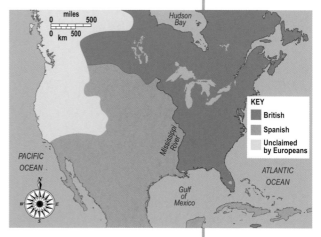

Moving Toward Rebellion

The cover shows how the *American Magazine* in 1758 addressed the concerns of colonists during the French and Indian War. A connection between the colonies was emerging, but it would be years before colonists discussed uniting as a nation.

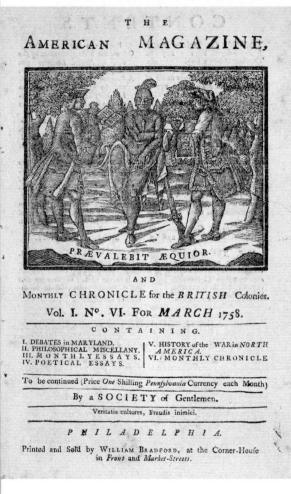

By 1763, the thirteen colonies were populated by an estimated 2.5 million men, women, and children, excluding the 500,000 Native Americans who also lived there. Colonists at this time willingly granted their allegiance to Britain, which had protected them during the French and Indian War. Within a decade, however, these formerly loyal subjects of King George III would be rebelling against his rule.

Taxing the Colonies

The French and Indian War left the British government with a large debt. The British thought the colonists need to pay more taxes as a contribution to the war's cost, and so Parliament passed the Sugar Act in 1764. This law put a tax on sugar, coffee, and other products the colonies **imported**. It also stopped them from importing goods from countries other than Britain. If they wanted the goods, therefore, American colonists had to pay the tax. A year later came the Stamp Act, which taxed all types of printed documents, from newspapers to playing cards.

The colonists were furious. They said the laws creating new taxes were unjust because the British colonies were not represented in Parliament. As British citizens, they felt they were entitled to elect the officials who made such laws.

Anger Grows

Groups of colonists calling themselves **Patriots** staged spirited—and sometimes violent—anti-tax protests. Some protesters hung straw dummies representing tax officials from trees. Other colonists **tarred and feathered** tax officials or destroyed their homes and offices.

It was not just taxes that angered the colonists. They were being prevented from moving onto lands west of the British colonies—territory recently claimed by Britain but inhabited by Native people. In 1763, in order to try and maintain peace with the Indian tribes who lived there, King George III made a proclamation forbidding white colonists—unless they had special permission—to settle on land west of the frontier that was

A Revolution of the Mind

"What do we mean by the [American] Revolution? The War with Britain? That was no part of the Revolution. It was only an effect and consequence of it. The revolution was in the minds of the people, and this was effected from 1760 to 1775, in the course of fifteen years before a drop of blood was drawn at Lexington."

John Adams, Massachusetts lawyer and Patriot,
after the American Revolution was over

Protests about taxes spread across the colonies. Here, the mayor of New York addresses an angry crowd.

Sons and Daughters of Liberty

The Sons of Liberty and the Daughters of Liberty were men and women in all thirteen colonies who protested against British taxation without representation in Parliament. The Sons of Liberty led protests against the Stamp Act of 1765 and, later, the Tea Act of 1773. The anger they felt over the laws sometimes exploded into violence, including tarring and feathering tax officials and other attacks. The Daughters of Liberty refused to buy tea and other British products so they would not have to pay any tax. They made tea from things like birch bark, sage, and rosemary and wore only clothes made in the colonies.

This grim cartoon in the *Pennsylvania Journal* used a skull and crossbones to show what colonists thought of the Stamp Act and the new taxes it created.

formed by the Appalachian Mountains. Resentment was still simmering because of this decree.

A Meeting of the Colonies

In October 1765, **delegates** representing nine colonies gathered in New York for the Stamp Act Congress. They pledged loyalty to the king but claimed the British Parliament did not have the right to tax the colonies without their approval. This meeting was an important step toward the colonies acting together.

The colonists believed they should have the right to elect representatives to Parliament because it was a right enjoyed by other British people. The phrase "no taxation without representation" became a rallying cry that led many colonists to oppose British rule. John Adams, a Boston lawyer and future U.S. president, argued: "The Stamp Act was made [in Parliament] where we are in no sense represented, therefore it is [not] binding upon us."

A Boycott and More Taxes

Patriots decided to **boycott** British goods. On November 1, 1765, the day the Stamp Act went into effect, everyone refused to buy

British ships arrive in Boston Harbor in 1768, full of soldiers sent to subdue rebellious colonists. The British navy was a powerful presence from the early days of the American Revolution.

items that were taxed. The boycott was so successful that Parliament canceled the tax—a huge victory for the colonists.

Despite colonial opposition to the Stamp Act, in 1767, Parliament passed the Townshend Acts, which taxed yet more goods: tea, paint, paper, lead, and other imported products. In response, violence against British officials increased again, and by 1768, the governor of Massachusetts decided he needed help. In September of that year, hundreds of British soldiers arrived in Boston.

Why and How People Pay Taxes

All governments, whether on a **federal**, state, or local level, need money to provide services to their citizens. Such services range from forming an army or police force to building roads and operating schools. Governments raise funds to pay for these services by asking their citizens to pay taxes.

People pay taxes based on the money they earn, the property they own, or the things they buy. The sugar tax and stamp tax were sales taxes—taxes paid on purchases—and this type of tax is still collected in many states today to pay for public services. In other states, people pay income tax—taxes on money they receive—as another way to cover the costs of these services. There was no federal income tax until 1862, when it was introduced to help the national government pay for the Civil War. Since 1913, income tax has been a regular source of funds for the federal government.

News of the Boston Massacre of 1770 was spread through the colonies by the publication of this engraving by silversmith Paul Revere. It is not accurate because it shows soldiers firing on a few peaceful civilians, when in fact there was an angry mob of hundreds of colonists.

The Liberty Song

"Come join in hand brave Americans all,
And rouse your bold hearts at fair Liberty's call;
No tyrannous acts shall suppress your just claim,
Or stain with dishonour America's name.
In Freedom we're born and in Freedom we'll live,
Our purses are ready,
Steady, Friends, Steady,
Not as slaves, but as Freemen our money we'll give."

John Dickinson, "The Liberty Song," Pennsylvania, 1768

The Boston Massacre

Patriots greatly resented the soldiers' presence, and the two groups often clashed. The most serious incident was the Boston Massacre, in which British soldiers fired on colonists for the first time. On the night of March 5, 1770, a soldier used his **musket** to strike a young boy who was taunting him. An angry crowd of some four hundred people quickly gathered to protest the incident. When eight other soldiers arrived to protect the first soldier, the crowd began to throw stones, rocks, and snowballs at the British. After a soldier panicked and accidentally discharged his musket, the other soldiers fired into the crowd. Five people were killed.

Repeal of the Townshend Acts

As colonists continued to boycott taxed goods, British businesses suffered because no one was purchasing their wares. In 1770, therefore, Parliament abolished the Townshend Acts, but it kept a small tax on tea as a point of principle. Many colonists were buying Dutch tea that was smuggled in, however, and the tea tax was mostly ignored. After the Townshend Acts were abolished, things calmed down for a while.

The Boston Tea Party

The peace did not last. In May 1773, Parliament passed the Tea Act. This law gave a British business, the East India Company, the right to sell tea directly to colonists without going through American tea importers. It angered colonists because the importers would lose their business if the East India Company sold their tea at a low cost, and because Americans who bought the tea would now be forced to pay the tea tax they opposed.

The Patriots did all they could to stop the distribution of the tea in the colonies. The most famous act of protest, known as the Boston Tea Party, occurred on December 16, 1773. Shortly after a Patriot meeting ended in Boston, the Sons of Liberty went to the harbor, boarded several ships, and tossed 342 chests of tea overboard.

The Sons of Liberty were rather badly disguised as Indians when they went aboard the British ships to destroy a shipment of tea. The action led to new more repressive laws, which in turn led to further acts of rebellion.

The Boston Tea Party enraged King George III. As ruler of Britain and its colonies, he believed that British North America belonged to him, and its people were his subjects.

The British Response

King George III vowed to make the colonists obey him. "The colonies," he said, "must either submit or triumph." In March 1774, Parliament passed several measures, which Patriots nicknamed the "Intolerable Acts." The laws were meant to punish colonists in Massachusetts and scare the other colonies into submission.

Under these Acts, Britain took military control of Massachusetts, and it restricted the power of the colony's legislature to make laws. The Acts also closed down the port at Boston and ordered Massachusetts to pay for the destroyed tea.

The Continental Congress

The Intolerable Acts further united the colonies against Britain. In September 1774, representatives from the legislatures of twelve colonies—only Georgia was absent—met in Philadelphia, Pennsylvania, at the first Continental Congress. Delegates criticized Britain for levying unfair taxes and limiting the colonies' right to govern themselves; and some even declared that Britain had no right to rule them. The colonies agreed to stop importing English products and to form local militia groups.

The Continental Congress was important because it showed that the various colonies were uniting in a common cause. In the opening session, Patrick Henry, a member of the Virginia legislature, made

A Plea to King George

"Kings are the servants, not the [owners] of the people. Open your breast, sire, to liberal and expanded thought. Let not the name of George the Third be a blot on the page of history."

Thomas Jefferson in an address to King George III, "A Summary View of the Rights of British America"

Benjamin Franklin (1706—1790)

Benjamin Franklin, a printer, publisher, inventor, philosopher, scientist, and diplomat, was one of the most brilliant colonial Americans.

Franklin was born in Boston and left school when he was only ten years old to work for his father, a candle and soap maker. He then became an apprentice in the printing trade and went on to become a successful publisher, first of the *Pennsylvania Gazette*, and then of the popular annual *Poor Richard's Almanac*.

Franklin was also an important scientist: he invented the lightning rod, a type of wood-burning stove, and bifocal glasses. In his older years, he was very influential in politics and in founding the United States of America. Franklin was one of the first people to suggest that the colonies should unite and work together for the common good. He represented the United States in Europe during the American Revolution, and after the war, he helped create the **Constitution**.

this clear by saying, "The distinctions between Virginians, Pennsylvanians, New Yorkers, New Englanders, are no more. I am not a Virginian but an American."

At the end of the Congress, the toast that began the farewell dinner was "May the sword of the parent never be stain'd with the blood of her children." But in just a few months, the first shots of

Delegates from the British colonies pray at the opening of the first Continental Congress in September 1774. The meeting was held in Carpenter's Hall, Philadelphia, and lasted for nearly two months.

the American Revolution would be fired at Lexington. It was there that the British "parent" would kill some of its colonial "children."

A Military Buildup

King George III was furious that colonists continued to defy him. He responded by sending more soldiers to Massachusetts, which Parliament claimed was in a "state of rebellion" against Britain. Boston, a city of sixteen thousand people, was now home to more than seven thousand **Redcoats**.

Militia groups, including Minutemen, began forming in Massachusetts and other colonies. These militias met several times

a week to train for war against the British. The Patriots also began storing weapons, gunpowder, and food so they could fight when the time came.

Ready for War

Although Massachusetts was the focal point of unrest, people in every colony were getting ready for war. Next to Massachusetts, Virginia was fiercest in opposing British rule. In March 1775, Patrick Henry gave a speech that summed up the attitudes of thousands of colonists. The most famous phrase from this historic address was "Give me liberty or give me death!"

In his famous speech of 1775, Patrick Henry warned that there would soon be military action in New England. Ten years earlier, Henry had made another famous speech, defending the rights of colonists to set their own taxes and comparing King George to tyrants in history.

A Cry for Liberty

"Gentlemen may cry, 'Peace! peace!'—but there is no peace. The war is actually begun! The next gale that sweeps from the north will bring to our ears the clash of resounding arms! Our brethren are already in the field! Why stand we here idle? What is it that gentlemen wish? What would they have? Is life so dear, or peace so sweet, as to be purchased at the price of chains and slavery! Forbid it, Almighty God! I know not what course others may take; but as for me, give me liberty or give me death!"

Patrick Henry, speech to the Virginia legislature, March 23, 1775

Chapter 3

At Lexington and Concord

Gage's Plan

General Thomas Gage, who commanded all British soldiers in the colonies and was also governor of Massachusetts, began to fear the many thousands of militiamen in his colony. In April 1775, Gage learned the Patriots, or **Rebels** as the British called them, were storing cannons, gunpowder, and food in Concord, which was 20 miles (32 kilometers) northwest of Boston.

Minutemen

The Minutemen in the American Revolution were storekeepers, teachers, doctors, farmers, and other ordinary people who claimed they could be "ready in a minute" to fight the British. These civilian soldiers were part of the local militia that grew rapidly in 1774 and 1775. They gathered together several times a week to train in how to march in formation, respond to battlefield commands, and load and shoot their muskets. Each Minuteman was required to have a musket, bayonet, and thirty-six rounds of ammunition. Some of them also carried hatchets, knives, and other personal weapons. Many of the Minutemen had fought in the French and Indian War, which gave them some combat experience. And because many colonists hunted wild game for food, they could shoot well.

Gage decided to seize the supplies. He also had orders from Britain to arrest the leading Patriots and send them to England so they could be tried on charges of **treason** for opposing British rule.

The most important leaders, Gage believed, were Samuel Adams, an organizer of protests and the cousin of John Adams; and John Hancock, a rich Boston merchant and prominent Son of Liberty. Hancock and Samuel Adams had just been elected as delegates to the Continental Congress. They knew they were in danger of arrest and were in hiding at the house of Hancock's relative, Reverend Jonas Clarke, in Lexington, 5 miles (8 km) from Concord.

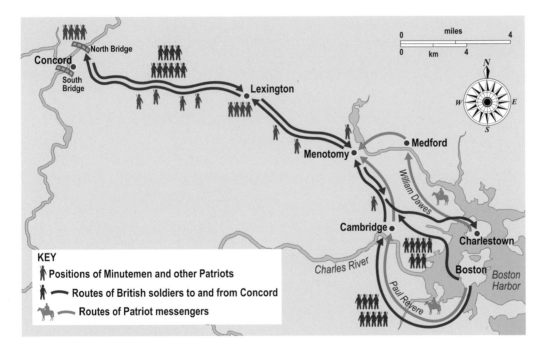

This map shows the area of Massachusetts where the American Revolution began in April 1775. Gage's plan was for British soldiers to leave Boston at night and head first to Lexington and then on to Concord. The map also shows the routes of two messengers sent to warn Patriots of the advancing British troops.

A Surprise Raid

Gage decided to send a large force—seven or eight hundred of his best soldiers—on a joint mission to arrest Hancock and Adams at Lexington and seize the arms at Concord. The British would be under the command of Lieutenant Colonel Francis Smith. Smith's second in command was Major John Pitcairn. Standing by, ready to follow if necessary, would be another commander, Hugh Percy, with one thousand men. To keep the raid secret, Gage told only his commanders where they were going, and he ordered that the soldiers leave at night.

Paul Revere's ride through the dark countryside and towns of Massachusetts has become a legend, partly due to a famous poem about the event by Henry Wadsworth Longfellow.

Paul Revere's Ride

". . . So through the night rode
Paul Revere;
And so through the night went his
cry of alarm
To every Middlesex village and farm,
A cry of defiance, and not of fear,
A voice in the darkness, a knock
at the door,
And a word that shall echo for
evermore!
For, borne on the night-wind of
the Past,
Through all our history, to the last,
In the hour of darkness and peril
and need,
The people will waken and listen
to hear
The hurrying hoof-beats of
that steed,
And the midnight message of
Paul Revere."

Henry Wadsworth Longfellow

The Rebels Respond

Patriot spies in Boston soon learned that the British were planning something. On April 16, 1775, Joseph Warren, a Patriot leader, sent Paul Revere, a courier for the Patriots, to Concord with a message to hide the weapons from the British. Warren then told Revere and William Dawes, another Patriot, to be ready to warn Hancock and Adams and raise the Minutemen when the soldiers left Boston.

The Night of April 18

On April 18, when they learned the soldiers were moving, the two messengers promptly set out by different routes to Lexington. Along the way, Revere alerted people that the British were marching toward them by shouting, "The Regulars are out!" and throwing gravel at people's windows. In Lexington, Revere woke up Adams and Hancock so they could escape. Joined by a third Patriot named Samuel Prescott, Dawes and Revere continued on toward Concord.

Between Lexington and Concord, the men were stopped by British patrols. Prescott escaped and rode on to Concord to warn the Patriots that the British were on their way.

Paul Revere (1735—1818)

Paul Revere was the son of French immigrant Apollos Rivoire, a metal worker, and learned from his father to be a goldsmith and silversmith. Revere took over the family business at the age of nineteen, when his father died.

Revere made a metal engraving of the Boston Massacre that helped dramatize that important incident. Prints of the engraving circulated widely and helped build support against British rule. He also served as a spy and courier for the Patriots before the American Revolution began. It was in this role that he made his famous ride.

During the American Revolution, Revere operated a gunpowder factory and was a major in a militia unit. After the war, he opened a foundry and the first copper rolling mill in the United States.

The British Reach Lexington

Lexington was a small community that consisted of several houses, a school, a church, and a few businesses. The town's buildings were grouped around a triangle of grass called Lexington Green. It was there that seventy or eighty Minutemen gathered in the early morning hours of April 19, 1775, waiting for the British to arrive. "Stand your ground!" Captain John Parker, the Patriot's leader, told the Minutemen. "Don't fire unless fired upon! But if they mean to have a war, let it begin here."

Colonial villages were often built around a central green. A rock on Lexington Green bears Parker's famous words.

At about 5:00 A.M., Major Pitcairn led the British troops into Lexington. Pitcairn was not looking for a fight either, and he had told his soldiers not to fire unless he personally ordered them to do so. A British officer, maybe Pitcairn, shouted at the Minutemen

gathered on Lexington Green: "Ye villains, ye rebels disperse! Lay down your arms!"

The First Shots

The heavily outnumbered colonists began to leave. Suddenly, a single shot rang out. No one knows who fired first; both the British and Patriots later claimed the other side was to blame.

After the shot was fired, hundreds of Redcoats began shooting at the Rebels with their muskets. The Minutemen returned fire as Pitcairn shouted, in vain, for his men to stop shooting. Within a few

On Lexington Green, gunfire opened quickly on both sides. When the smoke cleared, eight men had been killed.

minutes, Colonel Smith arrived and ordered a cease-fire, and the Redcoats reformed their ranks. Only one of the soldiers had been wounded, and the British soon set out for Concord.

They left behind a shocked town and a scene of blood and chaos. The British gunfire had killed eight Minutemen and injured ten others. One victim, Jonathan Harrington, lived near the scene

Patriots said they attacked the platoon on North Bridge, Concord, because they were afraid the British were going to burn the town. They may also have been acting in revenge for the killings at Lexington.

of the fight. Mortally wounded, he crawled to the doorstep of his home, where he died in front of his horrified wife and son.

Concord

At Concord, the people of the town had been busy hiding the Patriots' store of arms and ammunition when the British arrived about 8:00 A.M. The soldiers spread out: some were sent to guard North and South Bridges; others went to look for Rebel supplies in the town and on surrounding farms. The soldiers found and destroyed some wooden stands for cannons, setting fires that alerted more people in the surrounding area to their presence.

Meanwhile, militia members were gathering from nearby areas. By 10:00 A.M., several hundred Patriots had assembled around Concord. Seeing the smoke from the burning equipment, a large group of about four hundred men descended from a hill close to North Bridge. The British troops on the bridge fired some warning shots, but the men kept coming. A **volley** was fired from the British side: two Rebels were hit and died. The Patriots fired back, and within just a few minutes, three Redcoats were killed and at least nine others were wounded. The British platoon retreated into the town.

Not an Irregular Mob

"Whoever dares to look at them as an irregular mob will find himself very much mistaken. They have men amongst them who know very well what they are about."

Hugh Percy, commander of the British relief division on April 19, 1775

29

A replica of North Bridge at Concord now stands where the original bridge was in 1775.

The March Back to Boston

After regrouping in Concord, Smith and his officers decided it would be wisest to retreat. The number of colonists around the town was rapidly increasing, and Smith's main concern was how he would get his men back to Boston alive.

It was when the soldiers got about a mile outside Concord that the bloodiest part of the Battle of Lexington and Concord began. As the day wore on, the number of Rebels who came to fight increased until, eventually, there were well over three thousand men. Copying the tactics of Native Americans, small groups stationed themselves along the road from Concord to Lexington, shooting at the marching soldiers from windows and from behind trees, rocks, and stone walls. The British, who were trained to fight in solid ranks, became helpless targets as their column, now in chaos, straggled along several miles of road.

Relief Arrives

Percy's reserves arrived from Boston after a couple of hours, by which time the retreating soldiers had reached Lexington. Hundreds of Rebels continued to attack from every direction as the soldiers marched back to Boston. The British were now better protected, however, as they were gathered back into regiments, and Percy's men had fanned out on either side of the road, shooting every armed man they found. At Menotomy, about 5 miles (8 km) from Boston, 40 Redcoats and 40 Patriots died in the continued fighting.

By the end of the day, when the British troops finally reached safety in Charlestown, a town next to Boston, 73 soldiers had been killed and nearly 200 were wounded or missing. The Patriots had suffered about 50 fatalities and about 40 were reported wounded. There were probably more wounded who just went home. The first day of the American Revolution was over.

As the soldiers moved back along the road toward Boston, they were easy targets for the Rebels hiding behind fences and trees or in houses along the route.

Rebel Tactics

"[The Rebels fired] from all sides but mostly from the rear, where people had hid themselves in houses 'till we had passed, and then fired. The country was an amazing strong one, full of hills, woods [and] stone walls, which the Rebels did not fail to take advantage of, for they were all lined with people who kept an incessant fire upon us, as we did too upon them, but not with the same advantage, for they were so concealed there was hardly any seeing them."

British Lieutenant John Barker, describing Patriots attacking the
retreating British soldiers on the road to Boston, April 19, 1775

The War for Independence

The Second Continental Congress took place in Philadelphia at this building, now named Independence Hall. The Liberty Bell hung there, and it rang out in 1776 to celebrate the signing of the Declaration of Independence.

Notions of Liberty

"It is impossible to beat the notion of liberty out of these people. It is rooted in 'em from childhood."

British General Thomas Gage

Congress Meets

When the delegates to the second Continental Congress met in the city of Philadelphia in May 1775, they found themselves in a completely different situation than they had been in at their first meeting. Instead of discussing boycotts and writing petitions to the king, they were organizing the American Revolution.

George Washington Takes Command

The most important thing the Congress delegates did was to form an army, called the American Continental Army, and appoint George Washington of Virginia to lead it. In July 1775, Washington reached Boston, where thousands of militiamen were besieging the British inside the city. He was appalled by the ragged nature of the volunteers he would lead in battle. He wrote that "in a little Time we shall work up these raw Materials into good Stuff."

Washington camped near Boston and spent from July 1775 to March 1776 training his men. Meanwhile, fighting was taking place between Patriots and the British in other parts of North America, to the north and south of Massachusetts.

A Move for Independence and Unity

In Congress, a different battle was going on. The moderates were hoping to remain as a British colony once Britain started respecting their rights. Other delegates were moving toward the idea of

George Washington (1732—1799)

George Washington was born in Virginia as one of many children. At the age of eleven, after his father's death, he went to live at Mount Vernon, the plantation of his older brother. Washington later became an officer in the Virginia militia. He gained his first battle experience in the French and Indian War while serving as an aide to General Edward Braddock.

George Washington took command of the Continental Army at the beginning of the American Revolution and led American troops to victory. He then played an important role in drafting and helping pass the U.S. Constitution. Washington was elected as the nation's first president in 1789. In his eight years as president, Washington set a standard of excellence for every president who followed him. He returned to Mount Vernon after his retirement in 1797.

George Washington takes command of the Continental Army in 1775.

complete independence. And as more blood was shed in the Revolution, the moderates began to change their mind. In the spring of 1776, the individual colonies began to declare their independence and to talk of uniting themselves. In June, a group was appointed to prepare a declaration from the united colonies—called states from then on—to the rest of the world.

Thomas Jefferson (1743—1826)

Jefferson (right) with John Adams (center) and Benjamin Franklin (left), working on the Declaration of Independence.

Thomas Jefferson grew up in Virginia on a large plantation owned by his father. After attending college, Jefferson became a lawyer and then a member of the Virginia legislature. An eloquent writer, Jefferson was one of the most influential early leaders of the movement for independence for the colonies. His greatest contribution to his country was drafting the Declaration of Independence, a document that in future years would inspire independence movements in other countries. Jefferson became governor of Virginia in 1779 and went on to many other important offices: a senator in Congress (1783), an ambassador to France (1785), secretary of state (1789), and president of the United States (1801). He died on July 4, 1826, the fiftieth anniversary of the Declaration of Independence.

The Rights of Men

"We hold these truths to be self-evident, that all men are created equal, that they are endowed by their Creator with certain unalienable Rights, that among these are Life, Liberty and the pursuit of Happiness. That to secure these rights, Governments are instituted among Men, deriving their just powers from the consent of the governed."

From the Declaration of Independence,
Thomas Jefferson, 1776

The Declaration of Independence

Drafted by lawyer Thomas Jefferson, the Declaration of Independence listed the injustices the colonies believed Britain had committed. It also set forth an important idea, that governments derive their "just powers from the consent of the governed." This meant that officials could not make laws unless the people they governed gave them that power. If the government abused that power, citizens had the right to form a new government. The Declaration also stated that "all men" had basic rights.

Victories in New Jersey

The British had left Boston in March 1776 before Washington's army could attack them. Washington then moved his army to New York to capture that city. But his army was defeated and, in November, forced to retreat into New Jersey. A month later, the British pushed Washington farther west across the Delaware River into Pennsylvania.

Apparently defeated, Washington then took a daring gamble. Near midnight on December 25, 1776, he led his army back across the Delaware in a blinding snowstorm to attack Trenton, New Jersey. The Americans killed 22 British soldiers while only 4 of their own were wounded, took more than 900 prisoners, and seized badly

At a low point for the Patriots, Washington raised morale when he led his army across the Delaware River to make surprise attacks on British camps. This famous painting of the event is by Emanuel Leutze.

needed supplies. Washington surprised the British again with a similar raid on January 3, 1777, at Princeton, New Jersey.

British Victories

Washington still faced difficulties: his opponents were more experienced in battle, had a larger army, and were better equipped. The British, who rushed more troops to America and controlled the seas with their powerful navy, began to score major victories.

The winter of 1777 to 1778 was the low point of the war for American soldiers, who suffered greatly in their winter camp at Valley Forge, Pennsylvania. Without enough food and a lack of

Troops in the Patriot camp at Valley Forge huddle around a fire in cold weather, while Washington confers with his young French general, the Marquis de Lafayette (left).

warm clothes, as many as three thousand soldiers starved to death or died of disease at Valley Forge that winter.

Yorktown and Victory

In 1778, the situation began to improve for the Patriots. France signed a Treaty of Alliance with the United States and began sending supplies and troops to help the new nation fight. The number of Patriot soldiers increased, too, and in the next three years, Washington began to win battles. The victories helped Americans regain control of Pennsylvania and other areas held by the British.

In 1781, the British staged a massive invasion of the South. They overcame American forces in several battles, slashing their way through the former colonies to Yorktown, Virginia, a seaport. Washington moved his army south and trapped the British army, which was led by General Charles Cornwallis.

The siege of Yorktown began September 28. After several weeks of being shelled by American and French artillery, General Cornwallis decided he had no choice but to surrender. On October 19, 1781, he did so. With this American victory, the British government decided to stop fighting, and the war came to an end.

In this painting by John Trumball, Washington rides between lines of French and American troops during the British surrender at Yorktown on October 19, 1781. The victory of the rebellious colonists in the American Revolution rocked the monarchies of Europe.

A New Kind of Government

Chapter 5

Defeating Britain to win independence was only one part of the struggle that took place during the American Revolution. The second, equally difficult task for the United States of America was to create a system of government, one that would make the new nation strong while ensuring that citizens retained their rights.

Problems with the Articles

In 1781, the newly formed United States approved a document, the Articles of Confederation, which united the states economically and politically. The Articles had intentionally created a weak central government, for fear that a strong government would take control away from individual states, as Britain had done with the colonies.

The national government created by the Articles was so weak, however, that it could not govern properly. Many states, for example, refused to pay their taxes, which meant that federal officials did not have enough money to enforce laws and govern the nation.

Individual states also began fighting among themselves. One dispute was over ownership of land the United States had won from

This was the flag of the United States when it first became a nation, with a star and a stripe for each of the former colonies. At first, both stars and stripes were added for every new state, but in the early 1800s, Congress agreed to add stars every time a state joined the Union and keep the stripes permanently at the original thirteen.

The Revolution Continues

"There is nothing more common than to confound [confuse] the terms of the American Revolution with those of the late American War [for independence]. The American War is over: but that is far from the case with the American Revolution. On the contrary, nothing but the first act of that great drama is closed."

Dr. Benjamin Rush, a signatory of the Declaration of Independence

The Constitutional Convention, which lasted from May to September 1787, was an extraordinary and unique meeting. There, fifty-five leading American statesmen created a federal system of government, dividing power between the federal government and the individual states.

Britain but that was beyond the borders of the current states. Some states claimed their boundaries extended west to the Pacific Ocean.

The Constitutional Convention

When the states realized the Articles were not working, they decided to meet to create a better system of government. Delegates from every state gathered in May 1787 in Philadelphia for the

Constitutional Convention, at which a constitution was created for the United States.

Important Changes

The Articles had created a government—which kept the name "Congress"—but had not created an office for an individual leader because the former colonists feared that such a figure might become too powerful, like King George III. The Constitution did, however, create such a position: a president, or chief executive, would be the nation's most powerful elected official.

To balance the power of the president, two other branches of government were created. The legislative branch was called Congress and consisted of the House of Representatives and the Senate. These legislatures had the power to make laws. The judicial branch included the Supreme

The Constitution of the United States was approved on September 17, 1787. Much compromise was needed in the wording to get the necessary two-thirds of the delegates to sign.

We the People

"We the People of the United States, in Order to form a more perfect Union, establish Justice, insure domestic Tranquillity, provide for the common defense, promote the general Welfare, and secure the Blessings of Liberty to ourselves and our Posterity, do ordain and establish this Constitution for the United States of America."

Preamble to the United States Constitution, 1787

On February 4, 1789, George Washington was elected as the first president of the United States. His inauguration took place April 30, 1789, in New York City, then the nation's capital.

Court and other federal courts. This branch was given the power to decide whether the laws made were legal.

When voting began in 1787 on whether to **ratify** the Constitution, several states at first rejected it. Many Americans still feared giving so much power to the central government. In spite of these fears, on June 21, 1788, New Hampshire became the ninth state to approve the Constitution, and this approval provided the two-thirds majority needed for ratification. The Constitution would now become the law of the land.

The Bill of Rights

The new Congress of the United States met for the first time in March 1789. One of Congress's first steps was to add a Bill of Rights to the Constitution in order to address the concerns of many people. This took the form of amendments to the Constitution that guaranteed basic liberties. Ten amendments were approved, and on December 15, 1791, the Bill of Rights became part of the Constitution.

The First Amendment
"Congress shall make no law respecting an establishment of religion, or prohibiting the free exercise thereof; or abridging the freedom of speech, or of the press; or the right of the people peaceably to assemble, and to petition the Government for a redress of grievances."

First Amendment to the Constitution, Bill of Rights, 1791

41

Conclusion

Lexington and Concord Today

Today, visitors to the Minute Man National Historical Park can see where the first conflicts in the American Revolution took place. The sites of Lexington Green and North Bridge at Concord have been preserved together with several places along the route of the British retreat. The historical monuments remind us that the Rebels who fought here were, unknowingly, sowing the seeds of a new nation.

A New Age Begins

On June 2, 1782, the Continental Congress approved a Great **Seal** for the United States of America. One phrase on the back of the seal was taken from the words of the Roman poet Virgil. In Latin it reads *Novus Ordo Seclorum*. In English that means, "A new age now begins."

The new age for the United States was one that began with a new type of government, one that was aware of the importance of individual rights. There were many challenges ahead, however, if the nation was to live up to its own ideals, especially that of equality.

On the front of the Great Seal of the United States, the Latin motto translates as "Out of Many, One." This refers to the unification of the states.

An American

"He is an American, who, leaving behind him all his ancient prejudices and manners, receives new ones from the new mode of life he has embraced, the new government he obeys, and the new rank he holds. . . . The American is a new man, who acts upon new principles; he must therefore entertain new ideas and form new opinions. . . . This is an American."

J. Hector St. John de Crèvecoeur, Letters from an American Farmer, *1782*

The Legacy of Lexington and Concord

The most powerful phrase of the Declaration of Independence is "all men are created equal." However, equality was not created in the United States in 1776. The white men who led the country then had very different ideas about human rights than we do now. It would be many more years before all Americans would have a voice in how their country was governed. African-American slaves had no rights at all. Native Americans were also excluded from basic rights, and no women were allowed to vote. Voting was a right only for white males, and in many states, men also had to own property to be eligible to vote. Equality was a powerful promise to Americans, but one that would not come true for many decades.

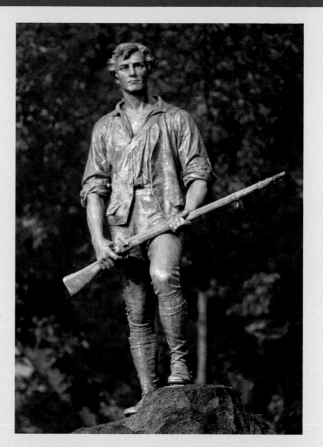

Minutemen are still considered heroes more than two hundred years after the American Revolution. This statue stands at Lexington to commemorate the Minutemen's contribution to American independence.

The Battle of Lexington and Concord left an important legacy, however, and not just for Americans but for other people around the world. The ideal that led to the first battle of the American Revolution—that of self-government as opposed to colonial or royal rule—spread to other countries and colonies. Over the last two hundred years, most monarchies have weakened or been abolished, and most colonies around the world have gained their independence.

Time Line

1754	■ French and Indian War begins.
1763	■ February 10: Treaty of Paris ends French and Indian War.
	October: King George III forbids British colonists to settle on Indian lands without permission.
1764	■ April 5: Parliament passes Sugar Act.
1765	■ March 22: Parliament passes Stamp Act.
	October: Stamp Act Congress condemns Stamp Act.
1767	■ Parliament passes Townshend Acts.
1768	■ September: Large number of British soldiers are sent to Boston.
1770	■ March 5: Boston Massacre.
1773	■ May 10: Parliament passes Tea Act.
	December 16: Boston Tea Party.
1774	■ March 24: Parliament passes first of "Intolerable Acts."
	September 5: First Continental Congress meets in Philadelphia.
1775	■ February: Parliament declares Massachusetts to be in state of rebellion.
	April 19: Minutemen and British soldiers clash at Lexington and Concord, beginning Revolutionary War.
	May 10: Second Continental Congress begins.
	July: George Washington takes command of American Continental Army.
1776	■ July 4: Congress approves Declaration of Independence.
	December 26: Battle of Trenton, New Jersey.
	January 3: Battle of Princeton, New Jersey.
1777	■ November 15: Congress approves Articles of Confederation.
1781	■ March 1: Articles of Confederation go into effect.
	September 28: Patriot troops surround Yorktown, Virginia.
	October 19: British army surrenders at Yorktown.
1783	■ September 3: Americans and British sign Treaty of Paris, formally ending Revolutionary War.
1787	■ May 25: Constitutional Convention opens in Philadelphia.
1788	■ U.S. Constitution is ratified.
1789	■ February 4: Washington is elected president of the United States and John Adams is elected vice president.
	March 4: First session of Congress of the United States.
	April 30: Washington is inaugurated as first U.S. president.
1791	■ Bill of Rights becomes part of U.S. Constitution.

Glossary

boycott: refusal to do business with a particular business or country in protest at its policies.

colony: settlement, area, or country owned or controlled by another nation.

congress: meeting. The name "Congress" was given to the first meetings of delegates from the British colonies and was then adopted as the name of the U.S. legislature when the United States formed an official government.

constitution: basic rules of government for a nation.

delegate: person chosen to represent a group at a meeting or in making decisions.

federal: having to do with the whole nation rather than separate states.

import: bring goods into a country, usually to sell. Imports were very important to colonial Americans, who got many of their household goods from Britain.

indentured servant: worker who agrees to work for a set period of time in exchange for an opportunity offered by an employer.

legislature: group of officials that makes laws.

militia: group of citizens organized into an unofficial army (as opposed to an army of professional soldiers).

Minutemen: special groups of militia who were ready to fight at short notice.

monarch: unelected ruler such as a king or an emperor. A system of government in which monarchs have the power to rule is called a monarchy.

musket: shoulder firearm common in colonial America and used during American Revolution.

natural rights: rights—including life, liberty, and the opportunity to acquire property—that many people in colonial America before the American Revolution believed were the basic rights of all people, which they were being denied.

Parliament: British legislature.

Patriot: colonist who supported the American Revolution; more generally, a person who is loyal to and proud of his or her country.

ratify: formally approve something by voting on it.

Rebel: colonist who supported the American Revolution; more generally, a person who fights against authority.

Redcoat: name for a British soldier, whose uniform included a red coat.

republican: to do with a republic, which is a nation led by elected officials and that has no monarch.

seal: stamp bearing an official symbol.

tar and feather: apply hot tar and feathers to the bodies of people as a very painful and often fatal form of punishment.

treason: crime of betraying one's nation.

volley: burst of gunfire.

Further Information

Books

Collier, Christopher and James Lincoln Collier. *The American Revolution, 1763–1783* (Drama of American History). Benchmark, 1998.

Knight, James E. *Boston Tea Party: Rebellion in the Colonies* (Adventures in Colonial America). Troll, 1998.

Martin, Joseph Plumb, George F. Scheer, editor. *Yankee Doodle Boy: A Young Soldier's Adventures in the American Revolution Told by Himself.* Holiday House, 1995.

Quackenbush, Robert. *Daughter of Liberty: A True Story of the American Revolution.* Hyperion, 1999.

Stein, R. Conrad. *The Declaration of Independence* (Cornerstones of Freedom). Children's Press, 1995.

Stratemeyer, Edward. *The Minute Boys of Lexington.* Lost Classics, 2001.

Web Sites

www.nps.gov/mima National Park Service web site has information about and pictures of the Battle of Lexington and Concord.

www.paulreverehouse.org Information from the Paul Revere Memorial Association about Revere and his role in the events leading to the Battle of Lexington and Concord.

www.wpi.edu/Academics/Depts/MilSci/BTSI/Lexcon Informative web site tells what happened at Lexington and Concord and has good links to more information: biographies, maps, and connected events.

Useful Addresses

Minute Man National Historical Park
174 Liberty Street
Concord, MA 01742
Telephone: (978) 369-6993

Index

Page numbers in *italics* indicate maps and diagrams. Page numbers in **bold** indicate other illustrations.

Adams, John, 15, 16, 25, **34**
Adams, Samuel, 25, 26
African Americans, 5, 11, **11**, 43
American Continental Army, 32, 33, **33**, 35, **35**, 36, **36**, 37, **37**
American Revolution, 5, 15, 21, 24, 27, 31, 32, 33, 35–37, 38, 43
  first shots of, 4, 21–22, 28, **28**, 42
Articles of Confederation, 38, 39

Bill of Rights, 41
Boston, 8, 10, 17, **17**, 18, **18**, 19, **19**, 20, 21, 22, 24, 25, 26, 30, 31, 32, 35
Boston Massacre, 18, **18**, 26, 30, 31
Boston Tea Party, 19, **19**, 20
Britain, 9, 12, 15, 38, 39
  American independence from, 5, 32–33, **34**, 38, 43
British colonies, 4, 5, 6–7, 8, *8*, 9, 10, 11, 12, 13, *13*, 14, 15, 20, 22, 24
  legislatures in, 9, 20, 23, 34
  religion in, 7, 8
  unification of, 16, 20, 21, 33, 38, **42**
  see also colonists
British government, 4, 9, 14, 25, 37
British soldiers, 4, **4**, 9, 12, 17, 18, **18**, 22, 24, 25, 26, 27
  at Battle of Lexington and Concord, 25, 28, **28**, 29, **29**, 30, 31, **31**
  during American Revolution, 32, 35, 36, 37

Champlain, Samuel, 13
Charlestown, 25, 31
Clarke, Jonas, 25

colonists
  early, 6–7, 8, 13
  lack of representation, 9, 14, 16, 33
  nationalities, 8, 9, 10, 11, 13
  protests by, 15, **15**, 16, 17, 18, **18**, 19, **19**, 20, 22, 23
  turn against Britain, 4, 14–23
  see also British colonies
Columbus, Christopher, 13
Concord, 4, 5, 24, 25, *25*, 26, 28, **29**, 29, 30, **30**, 42
"Concord Hymn," 5
Congress, 12, 34, 40, 41
  see also Continental Congress
Connecticut, 8, *8*, 10
Constitution, the U.S., 21, 33, 40, **40**, 41
Constitutional Convention, 39–40, **39**
Continental Army, *see* American Continental Army
Continental Congress, 25, 42
  first, 20, 21–22, **22**
  second, 32, **32**, 33
Cornwallis, Charles, 37

Daughters of Liberty, 16
Dawes, William, *25*, 26
Declaration of Independence, **5**, 32, 33, 34, **34**, 43
Delaware, *8*, 10

Emerson, Ralph Waldo, 4, 5

France and French colonies, 12, 13, 34, 37
Franklin, Benjamin, 21, **21**, **34**
French and Indian War, 12, 13, 14, 24, 33

Gage, Thomas, 24, 25, 32
George III, King, 4, 5, 14, 15, 16, 20, **20**, 22, 23, 32, 40
Georgia, *8*, 11, 20

Hancock, John, 25, 26
Harrington, Jonathan, 28
Henry, Patrick, 20–21, 23, **23**

"Intolerable Acts," 20

Jamestown, 6, **6**
Jefferson, Thomas, 20, 34, **34**

Lexington, 4, 22, 25, 25, 26, 27, **27**, 28,
    28, 30
Lexington and Concord, Battle of, 4, **4**, 5,
    25, 28–31, **28**, **29**, **31**, 42, 43
Lexington Green, **4**, 27, **27**, 28, **28**, 42
Longfellow, Henry Wadsworth, 26

Maryland, 8, 8, 10, 11
Massachusetts, 4, 7, 8, 8, 10, 17, 20, 22,
    23, 24, 25, **26**, 32
Menotomy, 25, 31
militia and militiamen, 20, 22–23, 24, **24**,
    27, 29, **29**, **31**, 32, 33
Minutemen, 4, **4**, 22, 24, **24**, 25, 26, 27,
    28, **28**

Native Americans, 5, 7, **7**, 12, 14, 15,
    30, 43
New Hampshire, 8, 8, 10, 41
New Jersey, 8, 10, 35, 36
New York City, 8, **10**, 13, **15**, 35, **41**
New York State, 8, 10, 16
North Bridge, 5, 25, 29, **29**, **30**, 42
North Carolina, 8, 8, 11

Paine, Thomas, 36
Parker, John, 27, **27**
Parliament, 5, 9, **12**, 14, 16, 17, 19, 22
    see also British government
Patriots, 15, 16, 18, 19, 24, 25, 26, 27, 32,
    35, 37
    at Battle of Lexington and Concord, 25,
    28, **28**, 29, 29, **30**, 31, **31**, 42

Pennsylvania, 8, 8, 10, 20, 32, 35, 36, 37
Percy, Hugh, 25, 30, 31
Philadelphia, 8, 10, 20, **22**, 32, **32**, 39, **39**
Pitcairn, John, 25, 27, 28
Plymouth, 7, **7**
Prescott, Samuel, 26
Puritans, 7, **7**, 8

Rebels, *see* Patriots
Redcoats, *see* British soldiers
Revere, Paul, **18**, 25, 26, **26**, 27
Rhode Island, 8, 8, 10

Smith, Francis, 25, 28, 30
Sons of Liberty, 16, 19, **19**, 25
South Carolina, 8, 8, 11
Spain and Spanish colonies, 13, *13*
Stamp Act, 14, 16, **16**, 17
Stamp Act Congress, 16
Sugar Act, 14, 17

taxes, 9, 14, 15, 16, 17, 19, 20, 23, 38
Tea Act, 16, 19
Townshend Acts, 17, 19
Treaty of Paris, 13, *13*

United States of America, 6, 27, 33, 42, 43
    founding of, 5, 21, 34, 38, **38**
    government of, 5, 38–41, 42, 43

Valley Forge, 36–37, **36**
Virginia, 6, **6**, 7, 8, 10, 11, 12, 20, 23, 32,
    33, 34, 36

Warren, Joseph, 26
Washington, George, 12, 33, **39**
    during American Revolution, 32, 33,
    33, 35, **35**, 36, **36**, 37, **37**, 38, **38**
    during French and Indian War, 12, 33
    as president, 33, **41**

Yorktown, 37, **37**